Hundreds of steps are negotiated while crossing a valley between Dizzard and Cleave (Stage 10)

South West Coast Path

6

Minehead to Porlock Wier
Start   South West Coast Path Monument, Minehead
Finish   Ship Inn, Porlock Weir
Distance   16km (10 miles)
Time   5hr

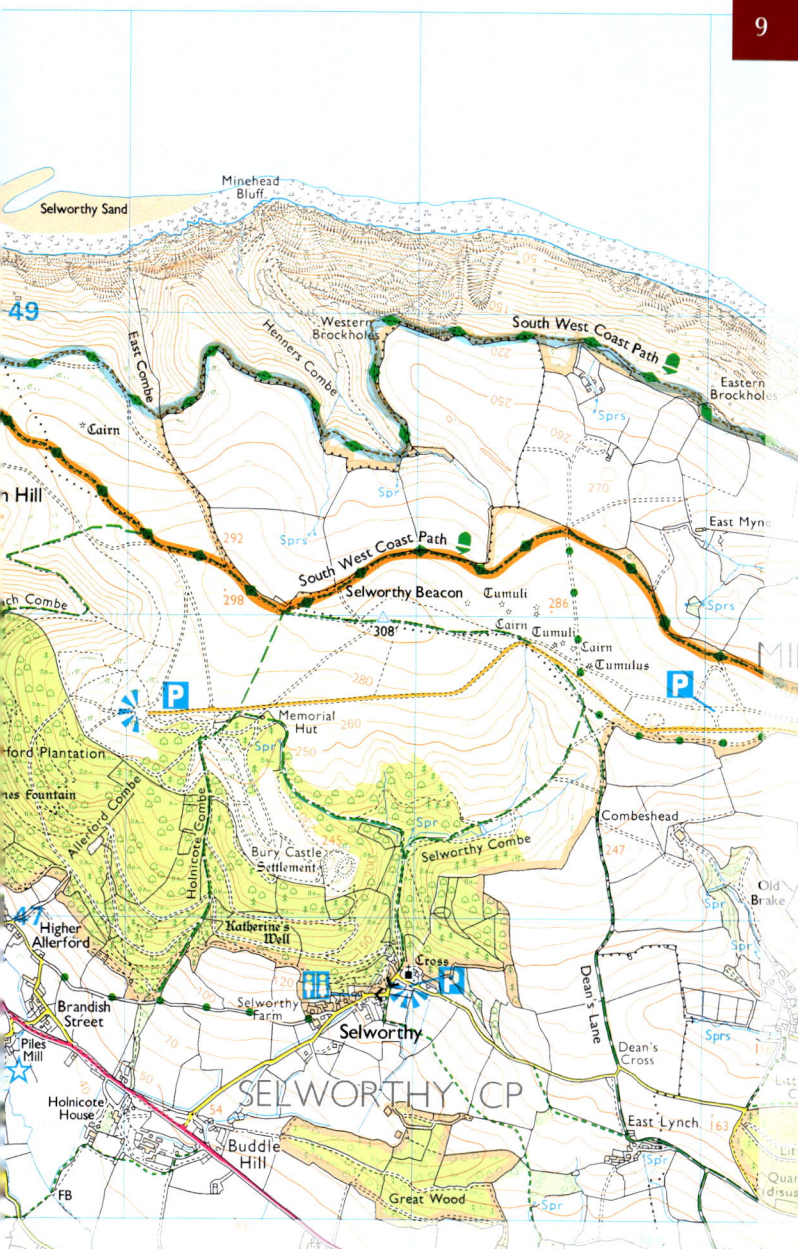

Porlock Wier to Lynmouth
Start Ship Inn, Porlock Weir
Finish Flood Memorial Hall, Lynmouth
Distance 18km (11 miles)
Time 6hr

11

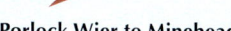

Porlock Wier to Minehead
Start   Ship Inn, Porlock Weir
Finish   South West Coast Path Monument, Minehead
Distance   16km (10 miles)
Time   5hr

13

15

Lynmouth to Combe Martin

Start	Flood Memorial Hall, Lynmouth
Finish	Royal Marine, Combe Martin
Distance	21.5km (13½ miles)
Time	6hr 30min

Lynmouth to Porlock Wier
Start   Flood Memorial Hall, Lynmouth
Finish   Ship Inn, Porlock Weir
Distance 18km (11 miles)
Time   6hr

18

20

21

The Mare and Colt

Red Cleave

Neck Wood

Waterfall

Hut Circles

Down

Sherrycombe

Path

Holdstone Down

261

The Glass Box
BSs
324

Trentishoe Barrows

TREN
Trentish

349
Holdstone Hill
Stones

Moorlands
Stones

MARTIN CP

Holdstone Farm
239

246

Trentis Manc

Rude Cotta

Vellacot Lane
263

262

Tattiscombe Farm

Woodend Cottage

273

270

Verwill Farm

Goulscott

Stony Corner
254

157

Coulsworthy

Combe Martin to Woolacombe
Start Royal Marine, Combe Martin
Finish Crossroads, Woolacombe
Distance 22.5km (14 miles)
Time 6hr

Combe Martin to Lynmouth
Start Royal Marine, Combe Martin
Finish Flood Memorial Hall, Lynmouth
Distance 21.5km (13½ miles)
Time 6hr 30min

24

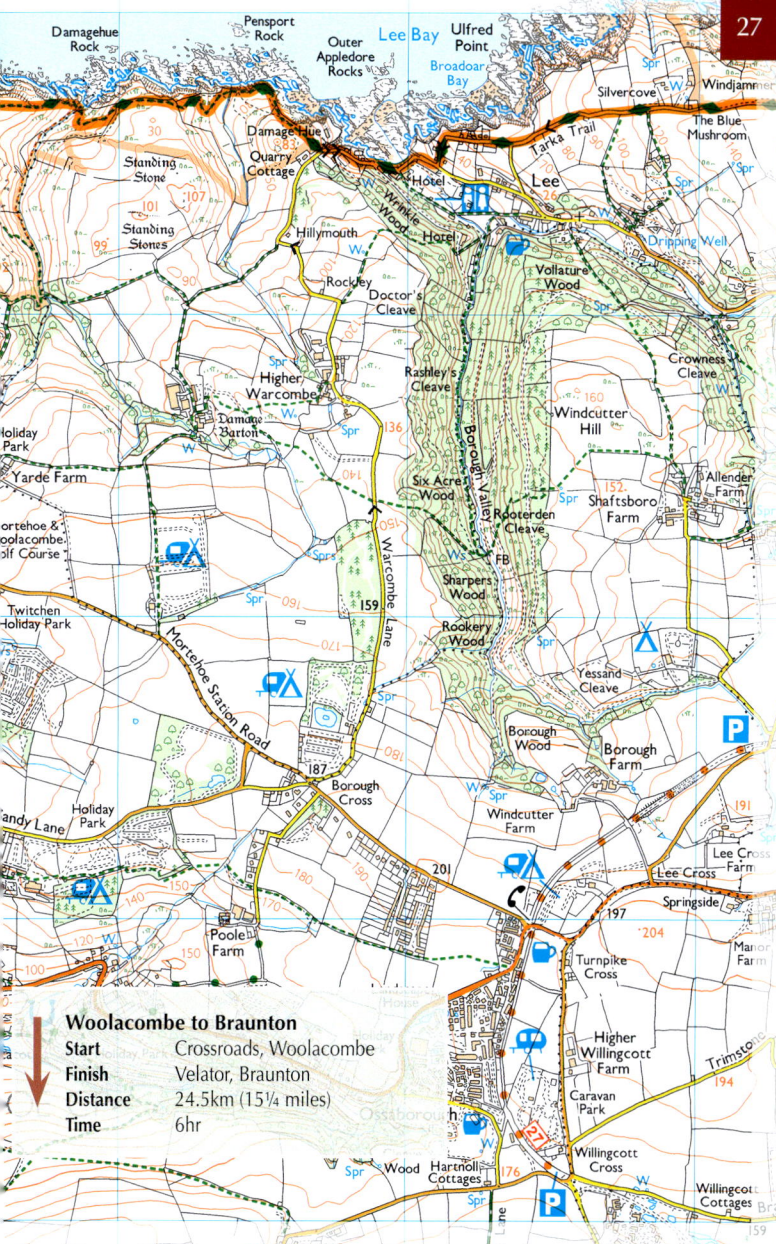

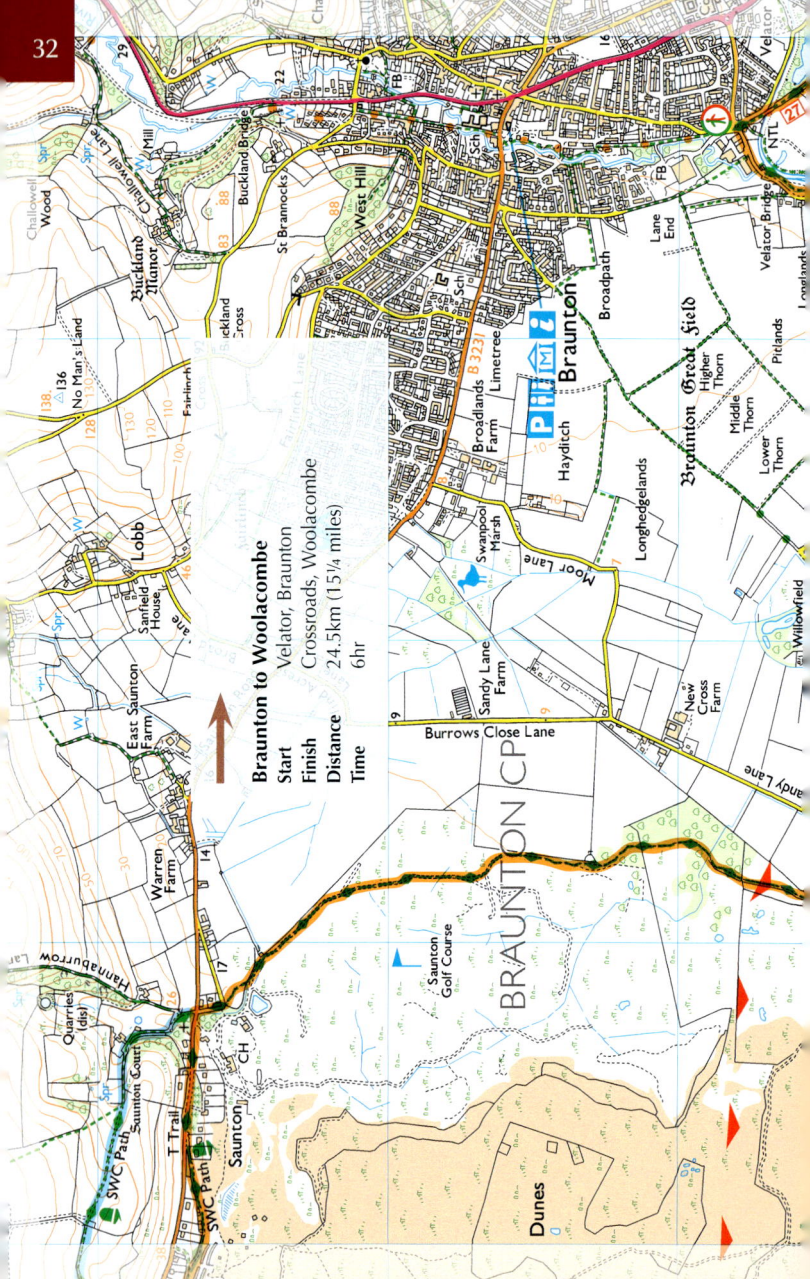

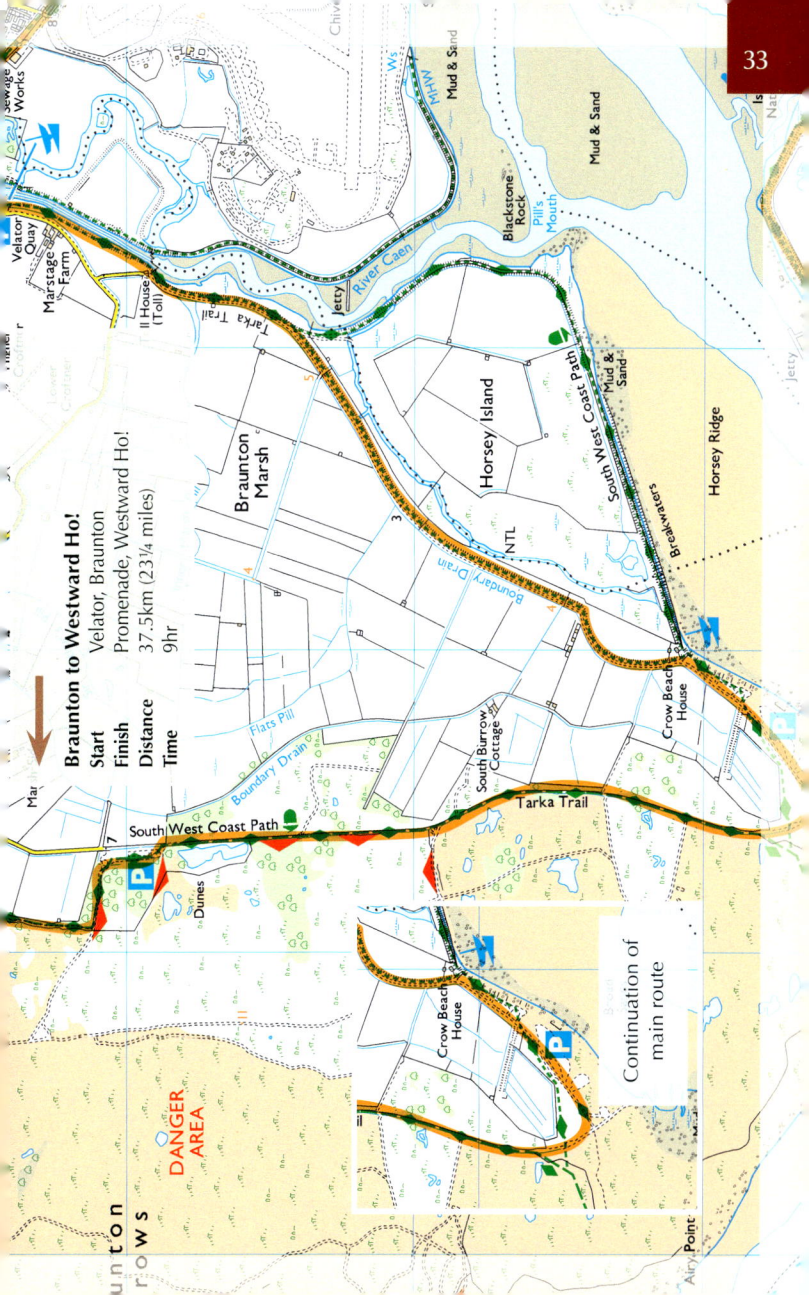

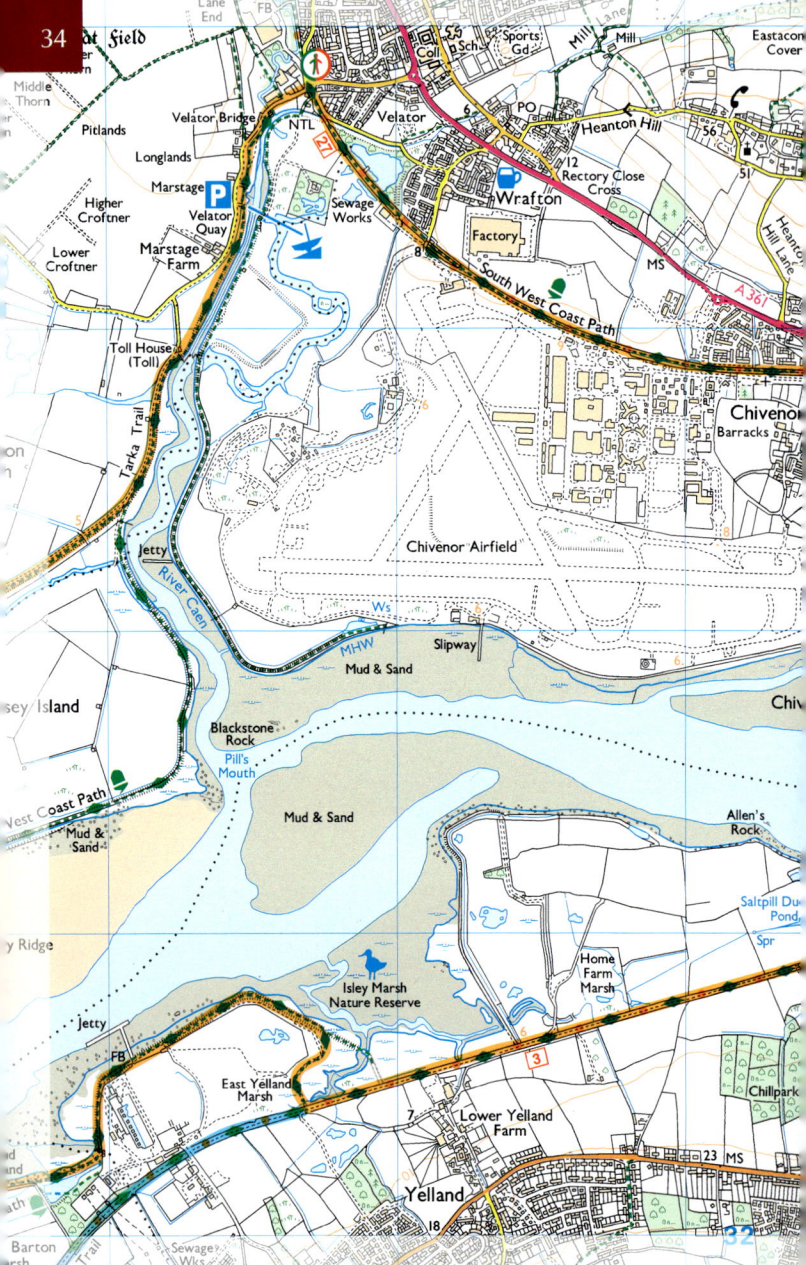

36

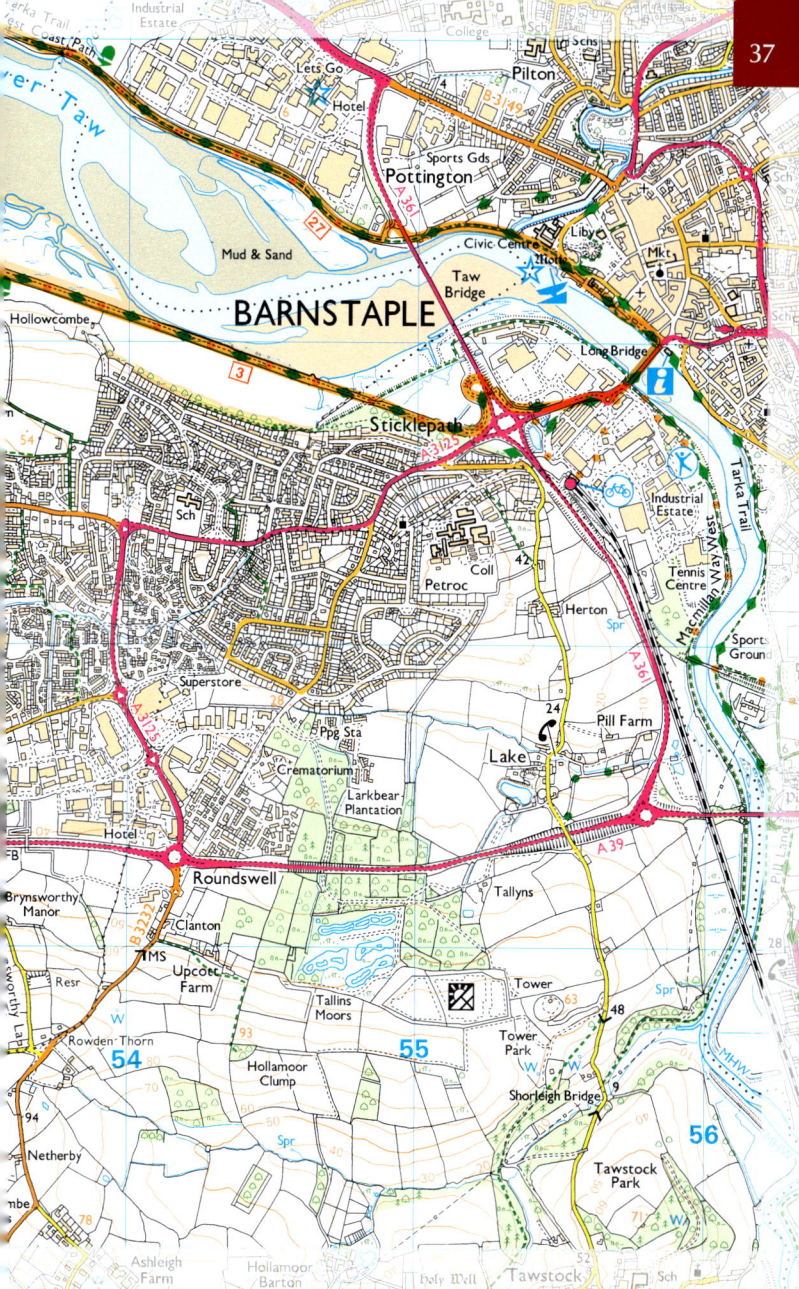

38

39

Map labels

- Slipway
- Mud & Sand
- MHW
- Chivenor Ridge
- Mud & Sand
- Mud & Sand
- Allen's Rock
- Fremington Rock
- Saltpill Duck Pond
- FB
- Spr
- 33
- MHW
- Isley Marsh Nature Reserve
- Home Farm Marsh
- Fremington
- PO
- Lower Yelland Farm
- Chillparks
- 23 MS
- Sch
- Yelland
- 32
- Leat Meadow
- West Yelland Farm
- Brake Plantation
- Broadmaid's Copse
- Cross Head
- Bickleton
- Moonacre
- 31
- Lydacott Farm
- Bickleton Cross
- CP
- Fullingcott Cross
- Little Knightacott Farm
- 49
- 50
- 51
- Fullingcott
- Beacon Farm
- Great Knightacott Farm
- Muxworthy Covert
- Collacott Farm
- Fullingcott Plantations
- Orchard Farm
- Lake Covert
- 30

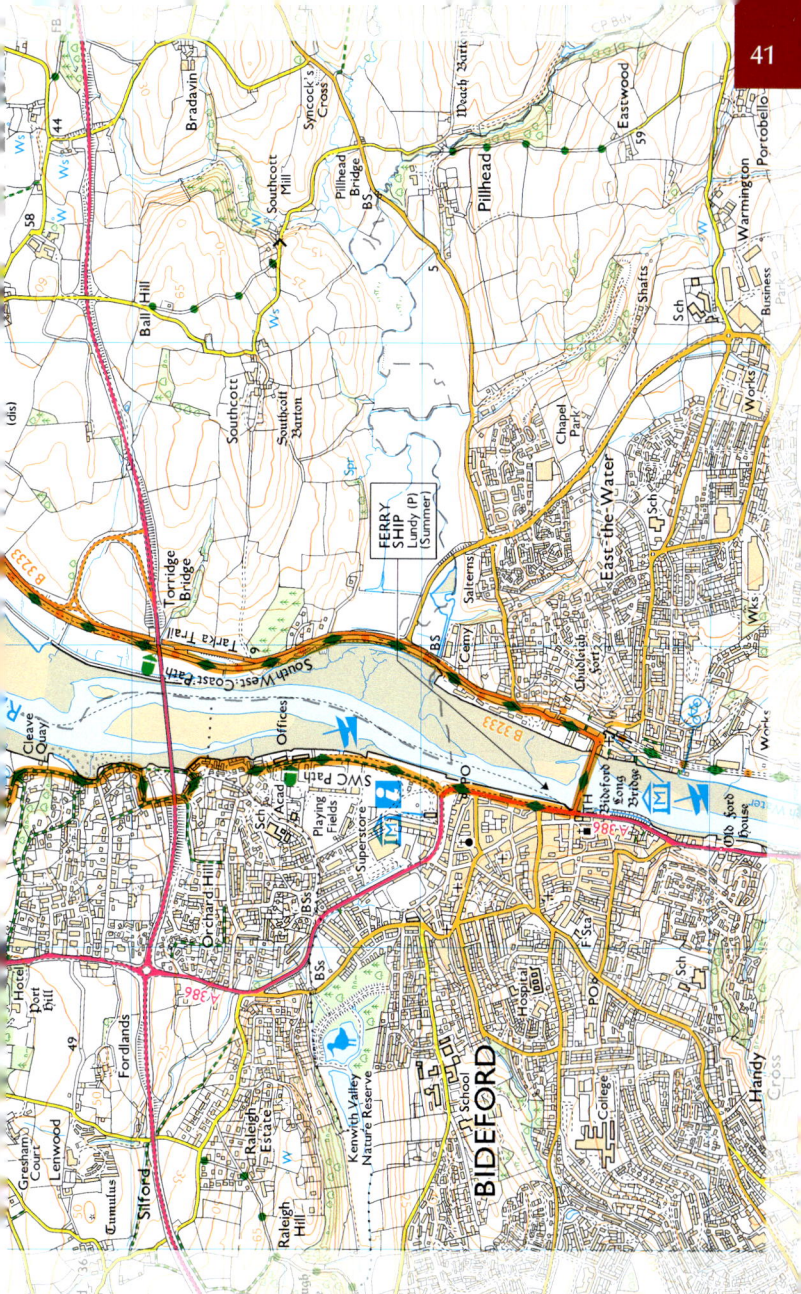

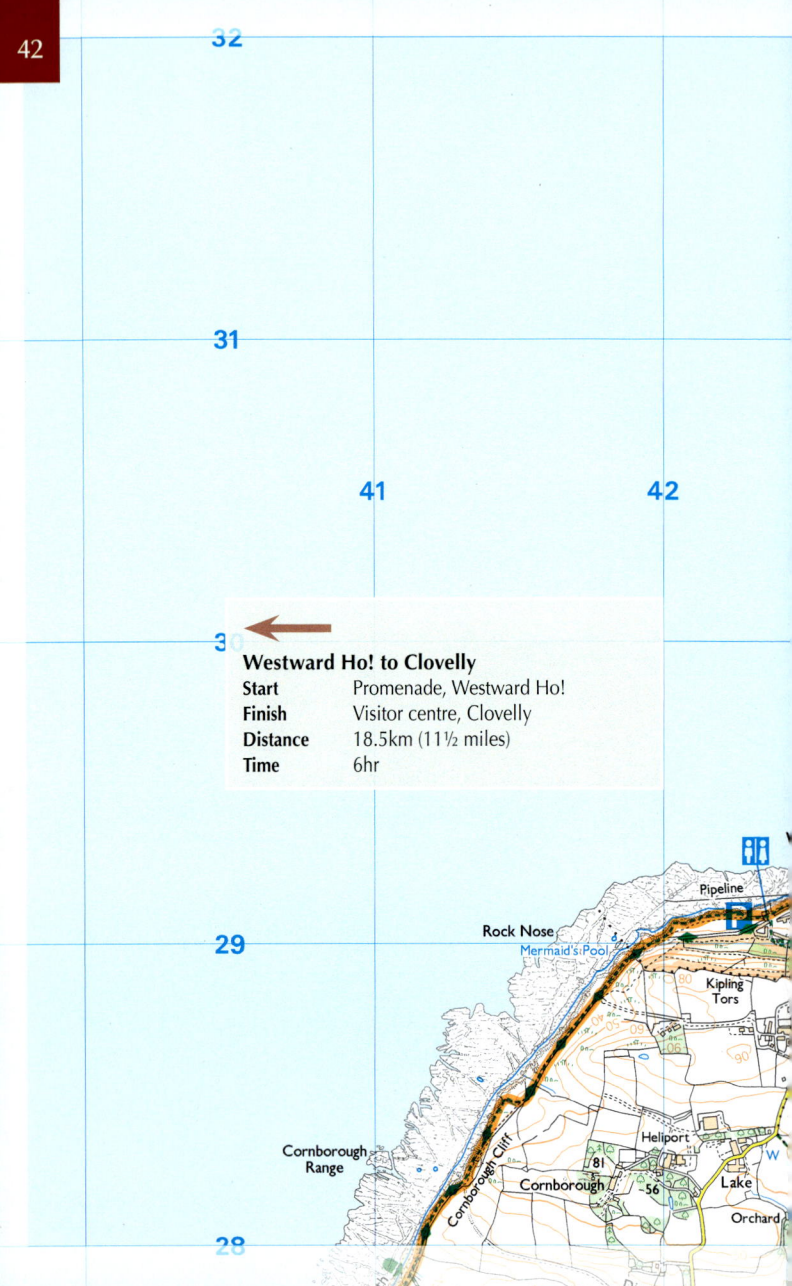

Westward Ho! to Clovelly

Start Promenade, Westward Ho!
Finish Visitor centre, Clovelly
Distance 18.5km (11½ miles)
Time 6hr

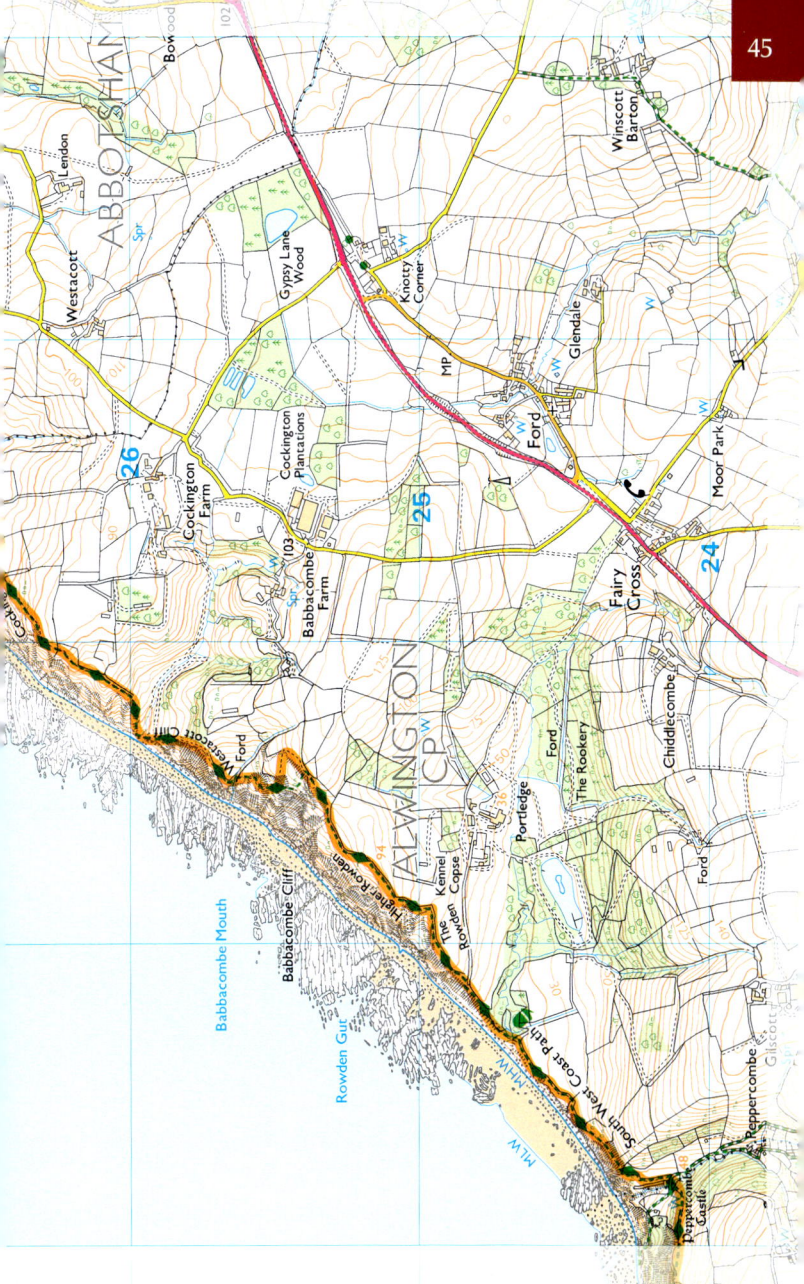

46

- Lower Bight of Fernham
- Mean High Water
- Mean Low Water
- The Gore
- Buck's Down
- Barton Wood
- Keivill's Wood
- The Hobby Drive
- South West Coast Path
- Sewage Works
- Quarry (dis)
- Hobby Lodge
- Buck's Barton
- Bideford Bay Holiday Park
- MP
- 198
- West Bucks
- A39
- PO
- Buck's Cross
- Cemy
- Downland Farm
- Reservoir
- Walland Farm
- North Bitworthy
- 208
- W Spr
- South Bitworthy Farm
- Garden Centre
- Kennerland Farm
- 195
- Galloping Lane
- Cranford
- Cranford Water
- Satchfield
- 201
- Sch
- PO
- 181
- Woolfardisworthy

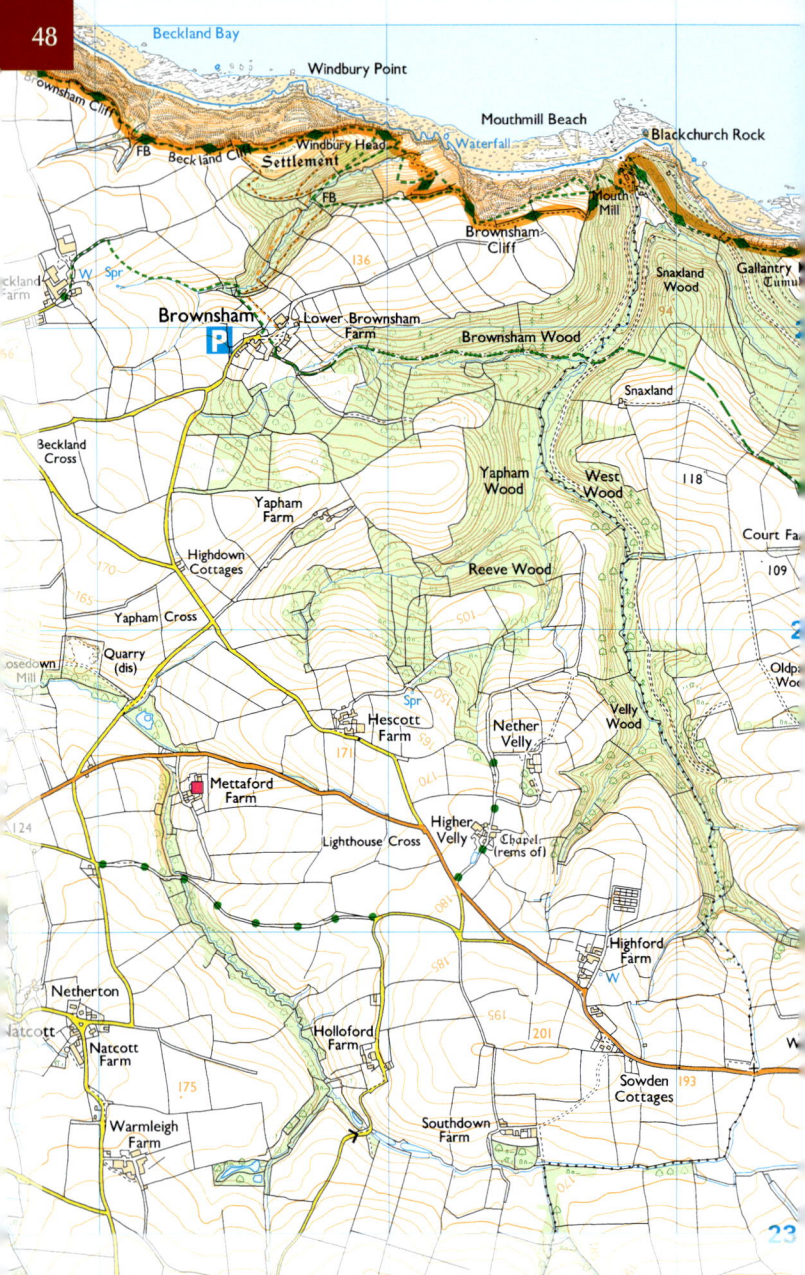

Clovelly to Westward Ho!
Start	Visitor centre, Clovelly
Finish	Promenade, Westward Ho!
Distance	18.5km (11½ miles)
Time	6hr

Clovelly to Hartland Quay
Start	Visitor centre, Clovelly
Finish	Hartland Quay Hotel
Distance	16.5km (10¼ miles)
Time	5hr

51

- Chapman Rock
- Little Chapman Rock
- South West Coast Path
- 152
- Exmansworthy Cliff
- 156
- West Fattacott Farm
- Fattacott Farm
- Exmansworthy
- Brownsham Cliff
- Beckland Bay
- Windbury Point
- FB
- Beckland Cliff
- Windbury Head
- Settlement
- FB
- 154
- Fatacott Cross
- 138
- Beckland Farm
- W Spr
- Brownsham
- Lower Brownsham Farm
- 136
- 166
- 150
- Beckland Cross
- Norton
- 119
- Yapham Farm
- Highdown Cottages
- Yapham Cross
- 165
- 150
- Rosedown
- Quarry (dis)

52

Hartland Quay to Clovelly

Start	Hartland Quay Hotel
Finish	Visitor centre, Clovelly
Distance	16.5km (10¼ miles)
Time	5hr

58

Bude to Hartland Quay
Start   River Neet, Bude
Finish   Hartland Quay Hotel
Distance   24.5km (15¼ miles)
Time   8hr

Bude to Boscastle
Start   River Neet, Bude
Finish   Youth Hostel, Boscastle
Distance   27km (16¾ miles)
Time   8hr 30min

62

Map labels

- East Dizzard
- Old Dizz
- Whitemoor
- Lufflands
- Chipark
- West Dizzard
- Dizzard Farm
- Higher Crannow
- West Crannow
- Coxford
- Higher Tresmorn
- Garth Vean
- Coxford Farm
- Dizzard Point
- Long Cliff
- Medieval village of Tresmorn (site of)
- Lower Tresmorn
- Chipman Strand
- Plane Rocks
- Chipman Point
- Waterfall
- South West Coast Path
- Waterfall
- Cleave
- Ford
- FB
- White Lodge
- Tel Ex
- Stoneivy Rock
- Chipman Cliff
- Scrade
- Mor's Hole (Cave)
- Cleave Strand
- Thorn's Beach
- St Gennys House
- Spr
- Gulf Rock
- Castle Point
- St Gennys
- Reservoir
- Churchtown Farm
- Crackington Haven
- Orchard Strand
- Fall
- FB
- Aller Shoot
- Little Barton Strand
- Great Barton Strand
- Pencannow Point
- Black Rock
- NTL
- Bray's Point
- Tremoutha Haven

Heights/spot values visible: 164, 149, 139, 147, 140, 138, 125, 136, 139, 87, 123, 134, 50, 136

63

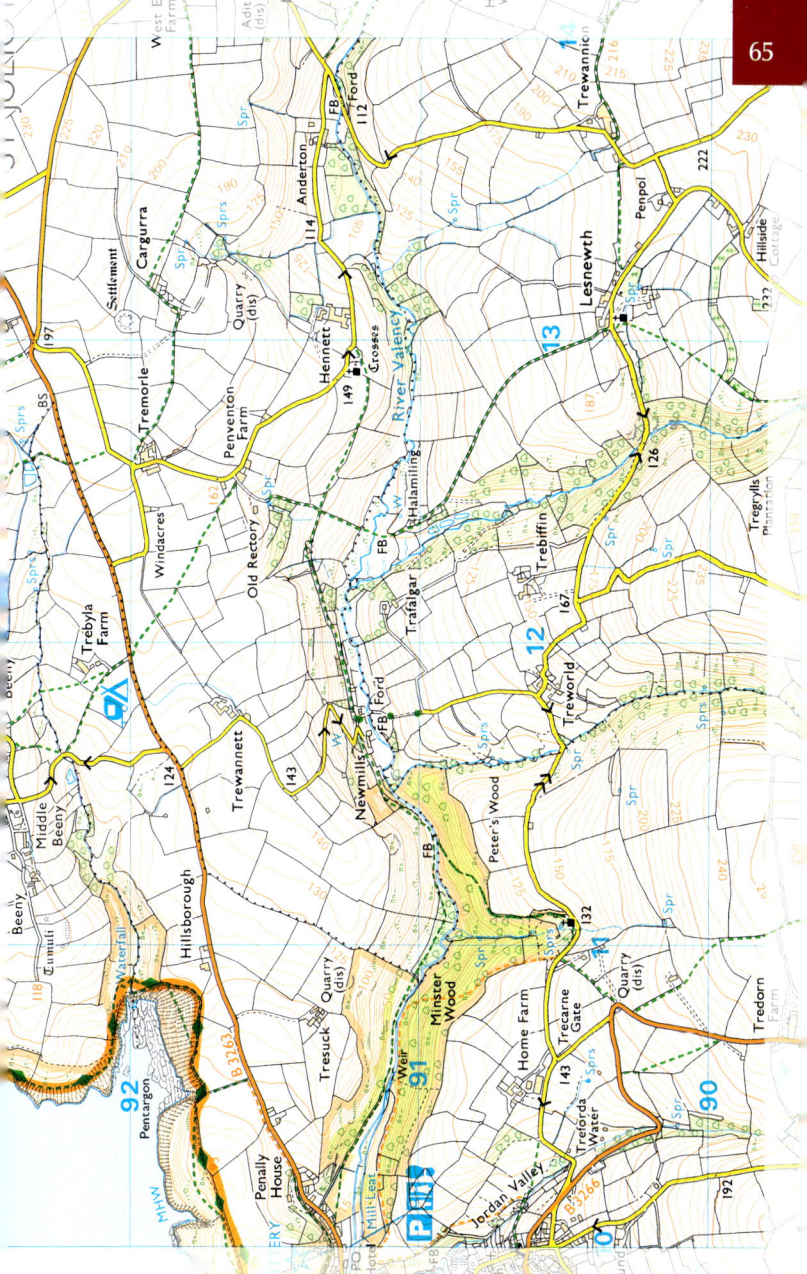

Boscastle to Port Isaac

Start	Youth Hostel, Boscastle
Finish	Harbour, Port Isaac
Distance	22km (13¾ miles)
Time	7hr

68

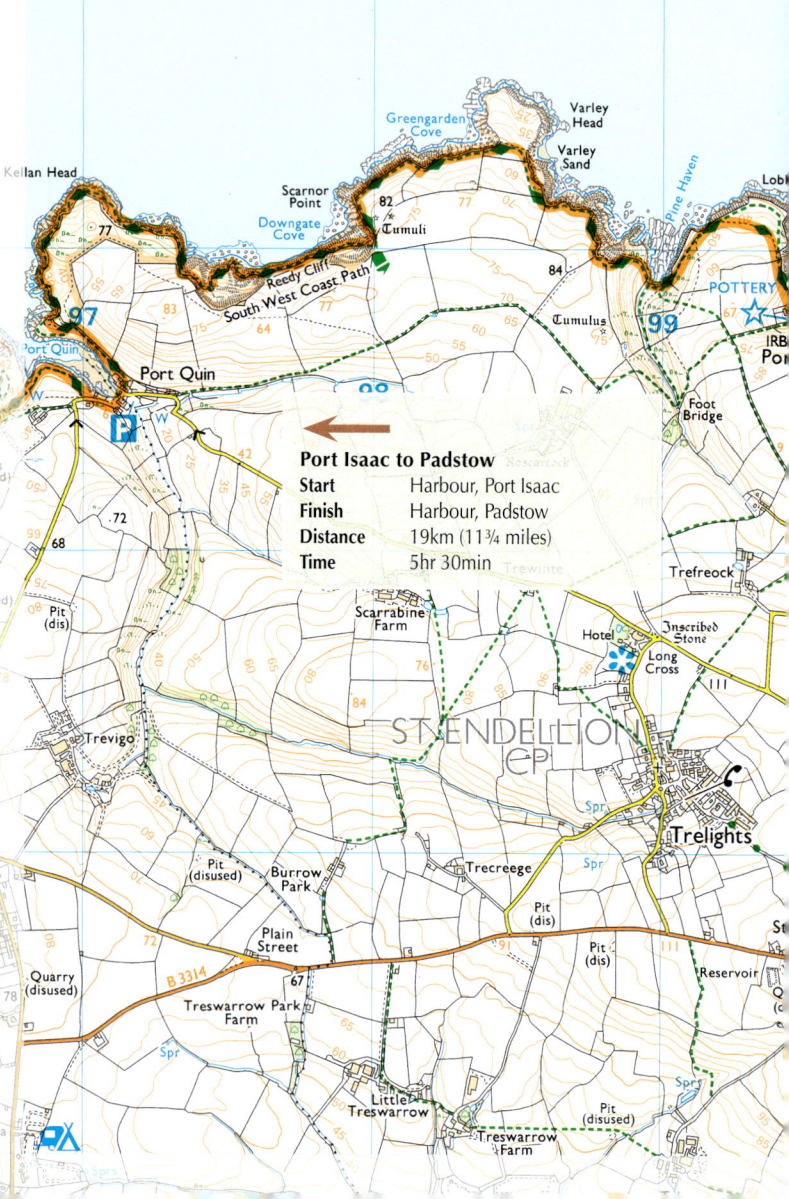

74

75

Kellan Head

Cow & Calf

Doyden Point

Port Quin Bay

95

96

Doyden Castle

97

Port

Pigeon Cove

Gibson's Cove

Carnweather Point

Trevan Point

Shafts (disused)

Downhedge Cove

Epphaven Cove

Great Lobb's Rock

Pennywilgie Point

Lundy Hole

Pit (disused)

Pit (dis)

Trevigo

Quarry (disused)

Porteath

BEE CENTRE

South Winds

Carruan

Green Close

Mesmear Farm

Quarry (disused)

Shaulders

Moyles

Treglines Farm

Pit (dis)

Roserrow

Gunvenna

Burial Ground

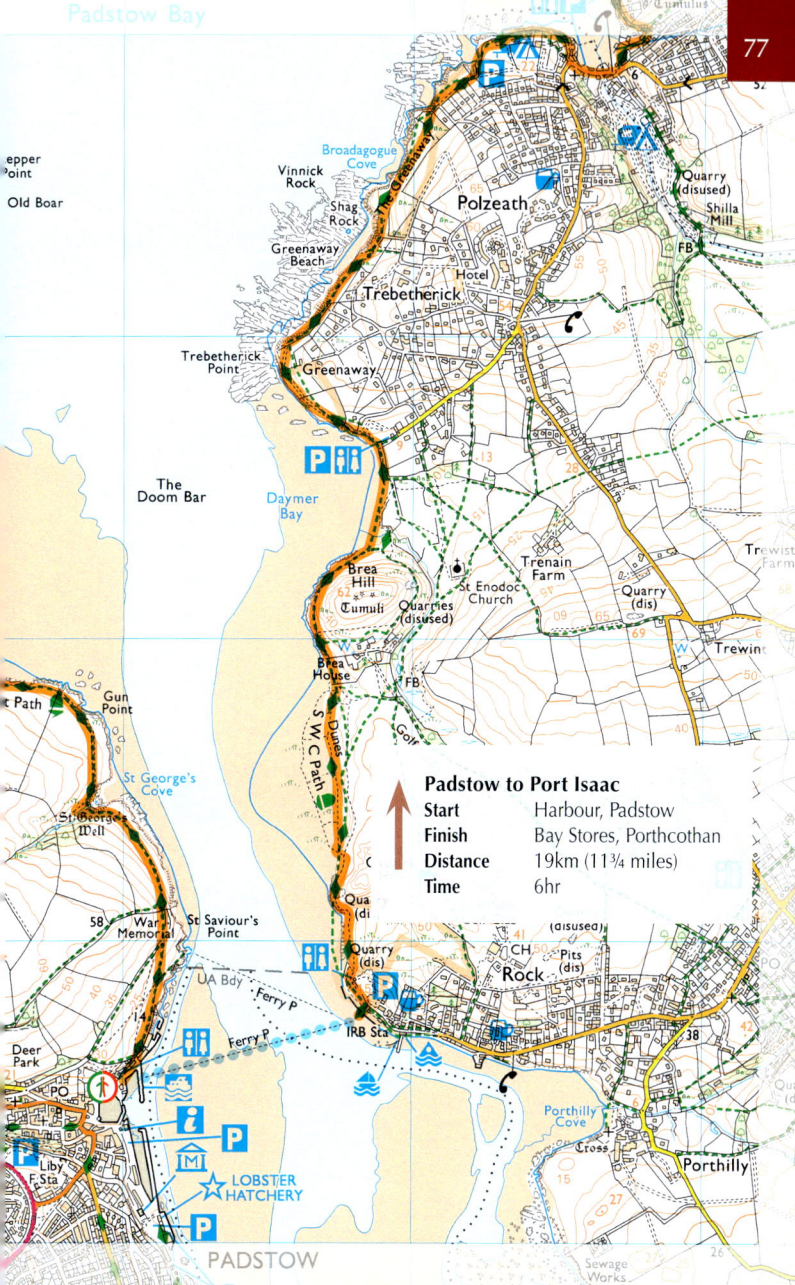

78

Porthcothan to Padstow

Start Bay Stores, Porthcothan
Finish Padstow Harbour, Padstow
Distance 22km (13¾ miles)
Time 6hr

Newquay to Porthcothan
Start   Harbour, Newquay
Finish   Bay Stores, Porthcothan
Distance 18km (11¼ miles)
Time   5hr

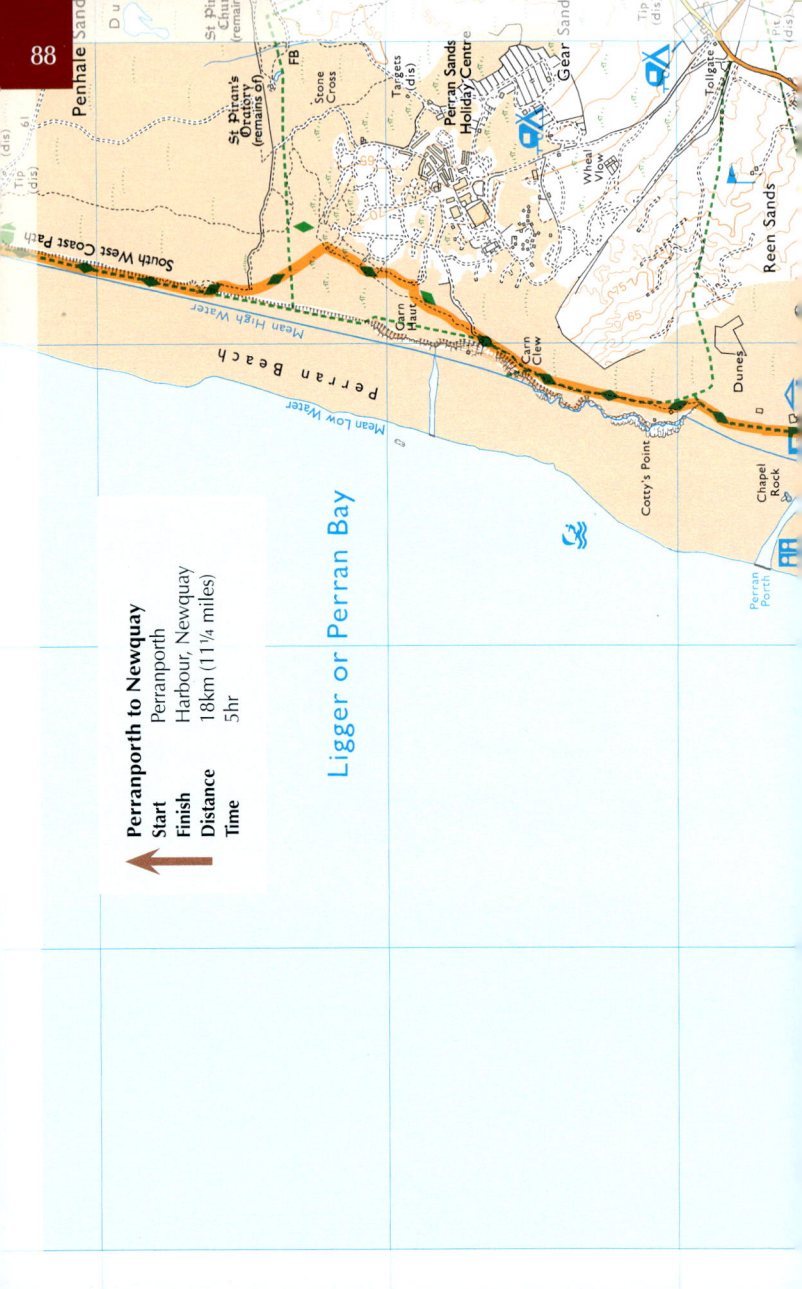

Portreath to St Ives
Start   Beach Car Park, Portreath
Finish   Porthmeor Road, St Ives
Distance 29km (18 miles)
Time   8hr

97

Castle Giver Cove
Fishing Cove
Hell's Mouth
Hudder Cove
Deadman's Cove
Derrick Cove
Cumulus
Hudder Down
B 3301
Butney Corner
Carlean Farm
Quarry (dis)
Red River Nature Reserve
Ashill
Reskajeage
Quarry (dis)
Gwealavellan
Settlement
Menadarva
Menadarva
Red River
Tip (dis)
Quarry (dis)
Quarry (dis)
Lower Trevorian Farm
Hillside
Kehelland
Nanterrow Farm
Ford
Nancemellin Farm
Bospebo Farm
Settlement
Trevorian
Quarry (dis)
Shaft (dis)
Nancemellin
Shaft (dis)
Quarry (dis)
Tip (dis)
Four La
Nanterrow Cottage
Nanterrow Lane
Fern Farm
Nancemellin Plantation
Tip (dis)
Chy
Cornhill Farm
Gwithian
Hope Farm
Merry Meeting

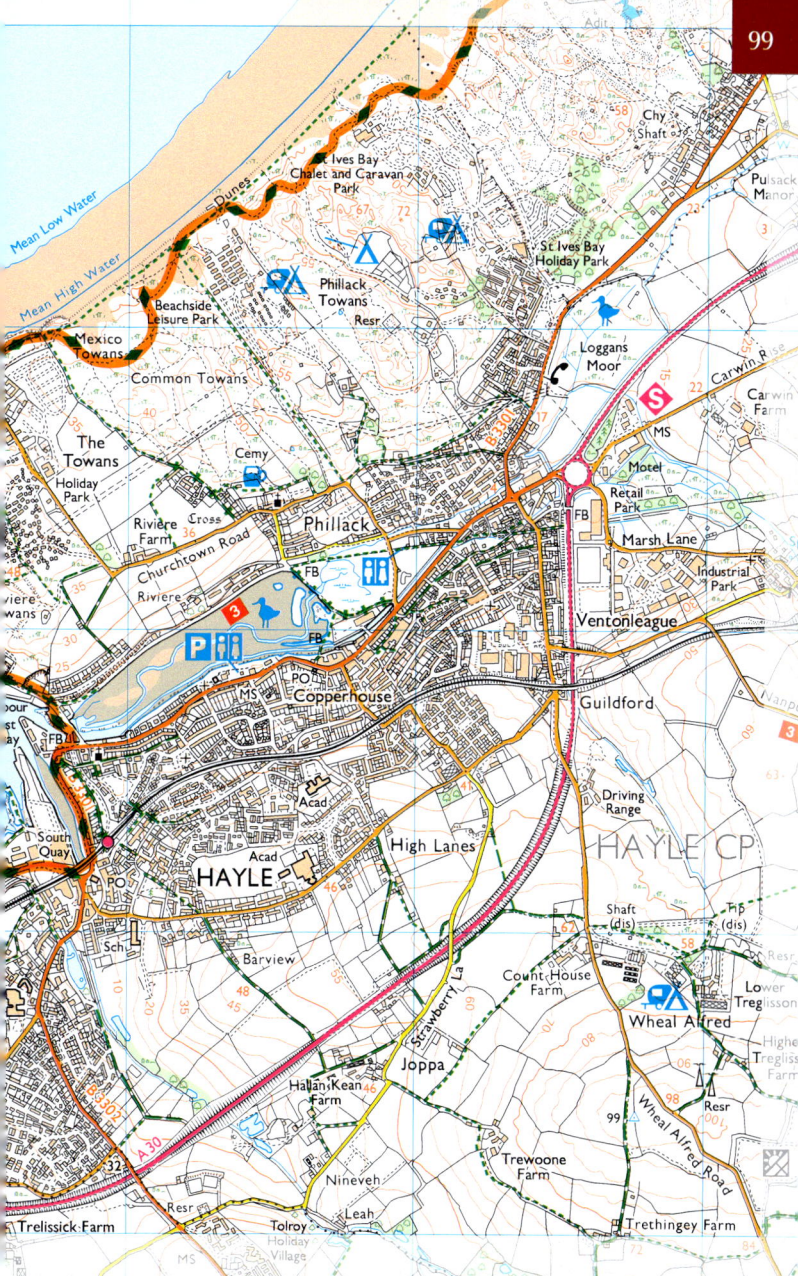

St Ives to Portreath

Start	Porthmeor Road, St Ives
Finish	Beach Car Park, Portreath
Distance	29km (18 miles)
Time	8hr

Approaching Trevaunance Cove in an area dotted with tin mines (Stage 16)

LEGEND OF SYMBOLS USED ON ORDNANCE SURVEY 1:25,000 (EXPLORER) MAPPING

ROADS AND PATHS — Not necessarily rights of way

M1 or A6(M)	Motorway
A 35	Dual carriageway
A30	Main road
B 3074	Secondary road
	Narrow road with passing places
	Road under construction
	Road generally more than 4 m wide
	Road generally less than 4 m wide
	Other road, drive or track, fenced and unfenced
» »	Gradient: steeper than 20% (1 in 5); 14% (1 in 7) to 20% (1 in 5)
Ferry	Ferry; Ferry P – passenger only
....	Path

- Service Area
- Service Area
- **7** Junction Number
- **T1** Toll road junction

RAILWAYS

- Multiple track / Single track — standard gauge
- Narrow gauge or Light rapid transit system (LRTS) and station
- Road over; road under; level crossing
- Cutting; tunnel; embankment
- Station, open to passengers; siding

PUBLIC RIGHTS OF WAY

- – – – – – Footpath
- — — — Bridleway
- + + + + + Byway open to all traffic
- – + – + – Restricted byway

The representation on this map of any other road, track or path is no evidence of the existence of a right of way

ARCHAEOLOGICAL AND HISTORICAL INFORMATION

Symbol	Description	Symbol	Description	Symbol	Description
✢	Site of antiquity	VILLA	Roman	☆	Visible earthwork
⚔ 1066	Site of battle (with date)	Castle	Non-Roman		

Information provided by English Heritage for England and the Royal Commissions on the Ancient and Historical Monuments for Scotland and Wales

OTHER PUBLIC ACCESS

• • • Other routes with public access — The exact nature of the rights on these routes and the existence of any restrictions may be checked with the local highway authority. Alignments are based on the best information available

♦ ♦ ♦ Recreational route

♦ ♦ ♦ 🚶 National Trail   ⓦ Long Distance Route

- - - - - Permissive footpath ⎫ Footpaths and bridleways along which landowners have permitted public use but which are not rights of way. The agreement may be withdrawn
— — — Permissive bridleway ⎭

• • • Traffic-free cycle route

[1] **1** National cycle network route number – traffic free; on road

ACCESS LAND

 Firing and test ranges in the area. Danger! Observe warning notices

 Access permitted within managed controls, for example, local byelaws. Visit **www.access.mod.uk** for information

England and Wales

 Access land boundary and tint

 Access land in wooded area

 Access information point

Portrayal of access land on this map is intended as a guide to land which is normally available for access on foot, for example access land created under the Countryside and Rights of Way Act 2000, and land managed by the National Trust, Forestry Commission and Woodland Trust. Access for other activities may also exist. Some restrictions will apply; some land will be excluded from open access rights. The depiction of rights of access does not imply or express any warranty as to its accuracy or completeness. Observe local signs and follow the Countryside Code.
Visit **www.countrysideaccess.gov.uk** for up-to-date information

BOUNDARIES

— + — + — National

— · — · — County (England)

— — — Unitary Authority (UA), Metropolitan District (Met Dist), London Borough (LB) or District
(Scotland & Wales are solely Unitary Authorities)

· · · · · · · · Civil Parish (CP) (England) or Community (C) (Wales)

━━━ ━━━ National Park boundary

VEGETATION

Limits of vegetation are defined by positioning of symbols

🌲🌲 Coniferous trees

🌳🌳 Non-coniferous trees

Coppice

Orchard

Scrub

Bracken, heath or rough grassland

Marsh, reeds or saltings

HEIGHTS AND NATURAL FEATURES

52 ·   Ground survey height
284 · Air survey height

Surface heights are to the nearest metre above mean sea level. Where two heights are shown, the first height is to the base of the triangulation pillar and the second (in brackets) to the highest natural point of the hill

HEIGHTS AND NATURAL FEATURES (continued)

Vertical face/cliff

Loose rock | Boulders | Outcrop | Scree

Contours are at 5 or 10 metre vertical intervals

- Water
- Mud
- Sand; sand and shingle

SELECTED TOURIST AND LEISURE INFORMATION

- Building of historic interest
- Cadw
- Heritage centre
- Camp site
- Caravan site
- Camping and caravan site
- Castle / fort
- Cathedral / Abbey
- Craft centre
- Country park
- Cycle trail
- Mountain bike trail
- Cycle hire
- English Heritage
- Fishing
- Forestry Commission Visitor centre
- Garden / arboretum
- Golf course or links
- Historic Scotland
- Information centre, all year
- Information centre, seasonal
- Horse riding
- Museum
- National Park Visitor Centre (park logo) e.g. Yorkshire Dales

- Nature reserve
- National Trust
- Other tourist feature
- Parking
- Park and ride, all year
- Park and ride, seasonal
- Picnic site
- Preserved railway
- Public Convenience
- Public house/s
- Recreation / leisure / sports centre
- Roman site (Hadrian's Wall only)
- Slipway
- Telephone, emergency
- Telephone, public
- Telephone, roadside assistance
- Theme / pleasure park
- Viewpoint
- Visitor centre
- Walks / trails
- World Heritage site / area
- Water activites
- Boat trips
- Boat hire

(For complete legend and symbols, see any OS Explorer map).

THE SOUTH WEST COAST PATH

This map booklet accompanies Paddy Dillon's guidebook to walking the South West Coast Path National Trail, from Minehead to South Haven Point. The guidebook features 1:50,000 OS mapping alongside detailed step-by-step route description and lots of planning and other information about local culture, wildlife and the protected coastline.

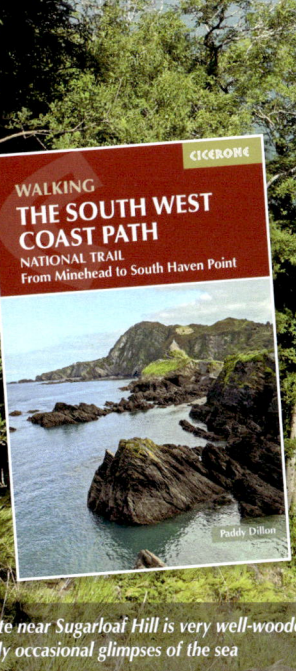

The route near Sugarloaf Hill is very well-wooded with only occasional glimpses of the sea

NOTES

NOTES

NOTES

LISTING OF CICERONE GUIDES

BRITISH ISLES CHALLENGES, COLLECTIONS AND ACTIVITIES
Cycling Land's End to John o' Groats
Great Walks on the England Coast Path
The Big Rounds
The Book of the Bivvy
The Book of the Bothy
The Mountains of England and Wales: Vol 1 Wales
The Mountains of England and Wales: Vol 2 England
The National Trails
Walking the End to End Trail

SHORT WALKS SERIES
Short Walks Hadrian's Wall
Short Walks in Arnside and Silverdale
Short Walks in Cornwall: Falmouth and the Lizard
Short Walks in Dumfries and Galloway
Short Walks in Nidderdale
Short Walks in Pembrokeshire: Tenby and the south
Short Walks in the South Downs: Brighton, Eastbourne and Arundel
Short Walks in the Surrey Hills
Short Walks Lake District – Coniston and Langdale
Short Walks Lake District: Keswick, Borrowdale and Buttermere
Short Walks Lake District: Windermere Ambleside and Grasmere
Short Walks on the Malvern Hills
Short Walks Winchester

SCOTLAND
Ben Nevis and Glen Coe
Cycling in the Hebrides
Cycling the North Coast 500
Great Mountain Days in Scotland
Mountain Biking in Southern and Central Scotland
Mountain Biking in West and North West Scotland
Not the West Highland Way Scotland
Scotland's Best Small Mountains
Scotland's Mountain Ridges
Scottish Wild Country Backpacking
Skye's Cuillin Ridge Traverse
The Borders Abbeys Way
The Great Glen Way
The Great Glen Way Map Booklet
The Hebridean Way
The Hebrides
The Isle of Mull
The Isle of Skye
The Skye Trail
The Southern Upland Way
The West Highland Way
The West Highland Way Map Booklet
Walking Ben Lawers, Rannoch and Atholl
Walking in the Cairngorms
Walking in the Pentland Hills
Walking in the Scottish Borders
Walking in the Southern Uplands
Walking in Torridon, Fisherfield, Fannichs and An Teallach
Walking Loch Lomond and the Trossachs
Walking on Arran
Walking on Harris and Lewis
Walking on Jura, Islay and Colonsay
Walking on Rum and the Small Isles
Walking on the Orkney and Shetland Isles
Walking on Uist and Barra
Walking the Cape Wrath Trail
Walking the Corbetts
  Vol 1 South of the Great Glen
  Vol 2 North of the Great Glen
Walking the Galloway Hills
Walking the John o' Groats Trail
Walking the Munros
  Vol 1 – Southern, Central and Western Highlands
  Vol 2 – Northern Highlands and the Cairngorms
Winter Climbs in the Cairngorms
Winter Climbs: Ben Nevis and Glen Coe

NORTHERN ENGLAND ROUTES
Cycling the Reivers Route
Cycling the Way of the Roses
Hadrian's Cycleway
Hadrian's Wall Path
Hadrian's Wall Path Map Booklet
The Coast to Coast Cycle Route
The Coast to Coast Walk
The Coast to Coast Walk Map Booklet
The Pennine Way
The Pennine Way Map Booklet
Walking the Dales Way
Walking the Dales Way Map Booklet

NORTH-EAST ENGLAND, YORKSHIRE DALES AND PENNINES
Cycling in the Yorkshire Dales
Great Mountain Days in the Pennines
Mountain Biking in the Yorkshire Dales
The Cleveland Way and the Yorkshire Wolds Way
The North York Moors
Trail and Fell Running in the Yorkshire Dales
Walking in County Durham
Walking in Northumberland
Walking in the North Pennines
Walking in the Yorkshire Dales: North and East
  South and West
Walking St Cuthbert's Way
Walking St Oswald's Way and Northumberland Coast Path

NORTH-WEST ENGLAND AND THE ISLE OF MAN
Cycling the Pennine Bridleway
Isle of Man Coastal Path
The Lancashire Cycleway
The Lune Valley and Howgills
Walking in Cumbria's Eden Valley
Walking in Lancashire
Walking in the Forest of Bowland and Pendle
Walking on the Isle of Man
Walking on the West Pennine Moors
Walking the Ribble Way
Walks in Silverdale and Arnside

LAKE DISTRICT
Bikepacking in the Lake District
Cycling in the Lake District
Great Mountain Days in the Lake District
Joss Naylor's Lakes, Meres and Waters of the Lake District
Lake District Winter Climbs
Lake District:
  High Level and Fell Walks
  Low Level and Lake Walks
Mountain Biking in the Lake District
Outdoor Adventures with Children – Lake District
Scrambles in the Lake District
  – North
  South
Trail and Fell Running in the Lake District
Walking The Cumbria Way
Walking the Lake District Fells –
  Borrowdale
  Buttermere
  Coniston
  Keswick
  Langdale
  Mardale and the Far East
  Patterdale
  Wasdale
Walking the Tour of the Lake District

DERBYSHIRE, PEAK DISTRICT AND MIDLANDS
Cycling in the Peak District
Dark Peak Walks
Scrambles in the Dark Peak
Walking in Derbyshire
Walking in the Peak District –
　White Peak East
　White Peak West

SOUTHERN ENGLAND
20 Classic Sportive Rides in
　South East England
　South West England
Cycling in the Cotswolds
Mountain Biking on the
　North Downs
　South Downs
Suffolk Coast and Heath Walks
The Cotswold Way
The Cotswold Way Map Booklet
The Kennet and Avon Canal
The Lea Valley Walk
The North Downs Way
The North Downs Way Map Booklet
The Peddars Way and Norfolk Coast Path
The Pilgrims' Way
The Ridgeway National Trail
The Ridgeway National Trail Map Booklet
The South Downs Way
The South Downs Way Map Booklet
The Thames Path
The Thames Path Map Booklet
The Two Moors Way
The Two Moors Way Map Booklet
Walking Hampshire's Test Way
Walking in Cornwall
Walking in Essex
Walking in Kent
Walking in London
Walking in Norfolk
Walking in the Chilterns
Walking in the Cotswolds
Walking in the Isles of Scilly
Walking in the New Forest
Walking in the North Wessex Downs
Walking on Dartmoor
Walking on Guernsey
Walking on Jersey
Walking on the Isle of Wight
Walking the Dartmoor Way
Walking the Jurassic Coast
Walking the South West Coast Path
Walking the South West Coast Path Map Booklets
　– Vol 1: Minehead to St Ives
　– Vol 2: St Ives to Plymouth
　– Vol 3: Plymouth to Poole
Walks in the South Downs National Park

WALES AND WELSH BORDERS
Cycle Touring in Wales
Cycling Lon Las Cymru
Great Mountain Days in Snowdonia
Hillwalking in Shropshire
Mountain Walking in Snowdonia
Offa's Dyke Path
Offa's Dyke Path Map Booklet
Ridges of Snowdonia
Scrambles in Snowdonia
Snowdonia: 30 Low-level and Easy Walks
　– North
　– South
The Cambrian Way
The Pembrokeshire Coast Path
The Pembrokeshire Coast Path Map Booklet
The Snowdonia Way
Walking Glyndwr's Way
Walking in Carmarthenshire
Walking in Pembrokeshire
Walking in the Brecon Beacons
Walking in the Forest of Dean
Walking in the Wye Valley
Walking on Gower
Walking the Severn Way
Walking the Shropshire Way
Walking the Wales Coast Path

INTERNATIONAL CHALLENGES, COLLECTIONS AND ACTIVITIES
Europe's High Points
Walking the Via Francigena Pilgrim Route – Part 1

AFRICA
Kilimanjaro
Walking in the Drakensberg
Walks and Scrambles in the Moroccan Anti-Atlas

ALPS CROSS-BORDER ROUTES
100 Hut Walks in the Alps
Alpine Ski Mountaineering
　Vol 1 – Western Alps
The Karnischer Hohenweg
The Tour of the Bernina
Trail Running – Chamonix and the Mont Blanc region
Trekking Chamonix to Zermatt
Trekking in the Alps
Trekking in the Silvretta and Ratikon Alps
Trekking Munich to Venice
Trekking the Tour du Mont Blanc
Trekking the Tour du Mont Blanc Map Booklet
Walking in the Alps

PYRENEES AND FRANCE/SPAIN CROSS-BORDER ROUTES
Shorter Treks in the Pyrenees
The Pyrenean Haute Route
The Pyrenees
Trekking the GR11 Trail
Walks and Climbs in the Pyrenees

AUSTRIA
Innsbruck Mountain Adventures
Trekking Austria's Adlerweg
Trekking in Austria's Hohe Tauern
Trekking in Austria's Zillertal Alps
Trekking in the Stubai Alps
Walking in Austria
Walking in the Salzkammergut: the Austrian Lake District

EASTERN EUROPE
The Danube Cycleway Vol 2
The High Tatras
The Mountains of Romania
Walking in Hungary

FRANCE, BELGIUM AND LUXEMBOURG
Camino de Santiago – Via Podiensis
Chamonix Mountain Adventures
Cycle Touring in France
Cycling London to Paris
Cycling the Canal de la Garonne
Cycling the Canal du Midi
Cycling the Route des Grandes Alpes
Mont Blanc Walks
Mountain Adventures in the Maurienne
Short Treks on Corsica
The Elbe Cycle Route
The GR5 Trail
The GR5 Trail – Benelux and Lorraine
The GR5 Trail – Vosges and Jura
The Grand Traverse of the Massif Central
The Moselle Cycle Route
The River Loire Cycle Route
The River Rhone Cycle Route
Trekking in the Vanoise
Trekking the Cathar Way
Trekking the GR10
Trekking the GR20 Corsica
Trekking the Robert Louis Stevenson Trail
Via Ferratas of the French Alps
Walking in Provence – East
Walking in Provence – West
Walking in the Ardennes
Walking in the Auvergne
Walking in the Briançonnais
Walking in the Dordogne
Walking in the Haute Savoie: North
Walking in the Haute Savoie: South
Walking on Corsica
Walking the Brittany Coast Path

GERMANY
Hiking and Cycling in the Black Forest
The Danube Cycleway Vol 1
The Rhine Cycle Route
The Westweg
Walking in the Bavarian Alps

IRELAND
The Wild Atlantic Way and Western Ireland
Walking the Wicklow Way

ITALY
Alta Via – Trekking in the Dolomites – Vols 1&2
Day Walks in the Dolomites
Italy's Grande Traversata delle Alpi
Italy's Sibillini National Park
Ski Touring and Snowshoeing in the Dolomites
The Way of St Francis
Trekking in the Apennines
Trekking the Giants' Trail: Alta Via 1 through the Italian Pennine Alps
Via Ferratas of the Italian Dolomites – Vols 1&2
Walking in Abruzzo
Walking in Italy's Cinque Terre
Walking in Italy's Stelvio National Park
Walking in Sicily
Walking in the Aosta Valley
Walking in the Dolomites
Walking in Tuscany
Walking in Umbria
Walking Lake Como and Maggiore
Walking Lake Garda and Iseo
Walking on the Amalfi Coast
Walking the Via Francigena Pilgrim Route – Parts 2&3
Walks and Treks in the Maritime Alps

MEDITERRANEAN
The High Mountains of Crete
Trekking in Greece
Walking and Trekking in Zagori
Walking and Trekking on Corfu
Walking in Cyprus
Walking on Malta
Walking on the Greek Islands – the Cyclades

NEW ZEALAND AND AUSTRALIA
Hiking the Overland Track

NORTH AMERICA
Hiking and Cycling the California Missions Trail
The John Muir Trail
The Pacific Crest Trail

SOUTH AMERICA
Aconcagua and the Southern Andes
Hiking and Biking Peru's Inca Trails
Trekking in Torres del Paine

SCANDINAVIA, ICELAND AND GREENLAND
Hiking in Norway – South
Trekking in Greenland – The Arctic Circle Trail
Trekking the Kungsleden
Walking and Trekking in Iceland

SLOVENIA, CROATIA, SERBIA, MONTENEGRO AND ALBANIA
Hiking Slovenia's Juliana Trail
Mountain Biking in Slovenia
The Islands of Croatia
The Julian Alps of Slovenia
The Mountains of Montenegro
The Peaks of the Balkans Trail
The Slovene Mountain Trail
Walking in Slovenia: The Karavanke
Walks and Treks in Croatia

SPAIN AND PORTUGAL
Camino de Santiago: Camino Frances
Coastal Walks in Andalucia
Costa Blanca Mountain Adventures
Cycling the Camino de Santiago
Cycling the Ruta Via de la Plata
Mountain Walking in Mallorca
Mountain Walking in Southern Catalunya
Portugal's Rota Vicentina
Spain's Sendero Historico: The GR1
The Andalucian Coast to Coast Walk
The Camino del Norte and Camino Primitivo
The Camino Ingles and Ruta do Mar
The Camino Portugues
The Mountains Around Nerja
The Mountains of Ronda and Grazalema
The Sierras of Extremadura
Trekking in Mallorca
Trekking in the Canary Islands
Trekking the GR7 in Andalucia
Walking and Trekking in the Sierra Nevada
Walking in Andalucia
Walking in Catalunya – Barcelona
Walking in Catalunya – Girona Pyrenees
Walking in Portugal
Walking in the Algarve
Walking in the Picos de Europa
Walking La Via de la Plata and Camino Sanabres
Walking on Gran Canaria
Walking on La Gomera and El Hierro
Walking on La Palma
Walking on Lanzarote and Fuerteventura
Walking on Madeira
Walking on Tenerife
Walking on the Azores
Walking on the Costa Blanca
Walking the Camino dos Faros

SWITZERLAND
Switzerland's Jura Crest Trail
The Swiss Alps
Tour of the Jungfrau Region
Trekking the Swiss Via Alpina
Walking in the Bernese Oberland – Jungfrau region
Walking in the Engadine – Switzerland
Walking in the Valais
Walking in Ticino
Walking in Zermatt and Saas-Fee

CHINA, JAPAN AND ASIA
Hiking and Trekking in the Japan Alps and Mount Fuji
Hiking in Hong Kong
Japan's Kumano Kodo Pilgrimage
Trekking in Tajikistan

HIMALAYA
Annapurna
8000 metres
Everest: A Trekker's Guide
Trekking in Bhutan
Trekking in Ladakh
Trekking in the Himalaya
Trekking in the Karakoram

MOUNTAIN LITERATURE
A Walk in the Clouds
Abode of the Gods
Fifty Years of Adventure
The Pennine Way – the Path, the People, the Journey
Unjustifiable Risk?
Unjustifiable Risk?

TECHNIQUES
Fastpacking
Geocaching in the UK
Map and Compass
Outdoor Photography
The Mountain Hut Book

MINI GUIDES
Alpine Flowers
Navigation
Pocket First Aid and Wilderness Medicine
Snow

For full information on all our guides, books and eBooks, visit our website:
www.cicerone.co.uk

CICERONE

Trust Cicerone to guide your next adventure, wherever it may be around the world...

Discover guides for hiking, mountain walking, backpacking, trekking, trail running, cycling and mountain biking, ski touring, climbing and scrambling in Britain, Europe and worldwide.

Connect with Cicerone online and find inspiration.

- buy books and ebooks
- articles, advice and trip reports
- podcasts and live events
- GPX files and updates
- regular newsletter

cicerone.co.uk